Assembled and rewritten by

Richard Hunt

BIGFOOT AND DOGMAN SIGHTINGS 3

Copyright © 2022 Richard Hunt

Be Aware

The stories within this book are eyewitness reports; hence Richard cannot substantiate the claims; however, he took every measure to ensure that these testimonies presented original and consistent details. Richard believes wholeheartedly in the following stories. Given that he, himself, has seen sasquatch, he's confident in his ability to detect the legitimacy of other reports.

Privacy Agreement

It's no surprise that so many people who submitted stories wish to keep their identities private. It's never been so easy to have your public image ruined by a mob of weak-minded individuals who do nothing but attack others on the internet. For that reason, I discouraged the ones who volunteered to share personal information, explaining that even if they didn't mind, they might have friends and family that could potentially face future ridicule.

Do You Have a Story to Tell?

I'm always looking for new bigfoot and dogman sighting reports. If you've seen these creatures in the flesh, please don't hesitate to send me an email with as many details as you can recall. I thank you in advance. You can write me at the following email address:

RichardHuntBigfoot@gmail.com

Contents

-Watched from the Woods-

Location: Dillard, Georgia

Submitted by: Connor A.

My family and I live just outside of Savannah, but we had a vacation home in Dillard that my wife and I inherited from my grandparents. One summer nearly twenty years ago, I was going through a rough time after losing my job and decided it was a good place to escape to. After about a week, it became clear that I was radiating tension nearly everywhere I went, even while around my two daughters, who were only nine and seven at the time. My wife was the one who came up with the idea that I should spend some time alone in Dillard. She believed the fresh air and solitude would help me clear my mind and maybe decide my next step. I wasn't all that enthusiastic about the idea, but I didn't have any of my own, so I decided to give it a trial of at least a few days. The drive is over five hours, and I've always gotten a little antsy during long road trips, but I sucked it up.

Soon after arriving at our house in Dillard, I immediately noticed various things that needed fixing. Getting distracted right away turned out to be a good thing. Crafts of any kind have always been a stress-reliever for me. I love working with my hands. After a couple of days, I wondered how I had ever suffered through an office job. I'm just not cut out for that sort of thing, but I fell into it anyway. Where had I gone wrong?

Scrap wood accumulated with every project I finished, and I wondered where I could put it to use. After replacing an old workbench within the shed, I hauled the piece of junk out to a shaded space deep in the backyard. I thought it would be an excellent place to continue my work after overheating inside the shed. The shed had poor ventilation, so I'd usually start sweating bullets once early afternoon rolled around. There was one time I was so focused on a task that I stayed in there for way too long and felt like I was on the verge of heatstroke. It was scary stuff, but not nearly as frightening as what I spotted one day on the edge of the property.

A few days earlier, I started using some of the scrap wood to make a new birdhouse after I came across one that was falling apart. I then impulsively decided that I'd make several of them and deliver them to the neighbors—the closest one being at least 200 yards away. It seemed like a smart way to get on the neighbors' good side so that they'd keep their eyes on our property since our family was rarely around. One of the nicest things about the houses in that area was how they came with a few acres. Plenty of trees made it a great place for wild animals to roam. There was plenty of deer and other mammals around, and I think that's why the strange creature hung out there.

I believe I was working on my third treehouse when I noticed a dark figure peeking at me from behind a tree. I could see about half of its head and maybe a third of its torso. At first, I thought it was someone wearing a black sweatshirt and a black ski mask—like how robbers and burglars often look in the movies. But it only took me a few seconds to grasp that this was no human; it looked like a monkey with an extra-wide mouth and big round eyes.

Although we were looking at one another, I couldn't make up my mind on how to act. I wondered if it might attack me if I spoke to it. We were still a considerable distance apart, so I would've had to shout to talk to it. I didn't want to risk it confusing that for a roar or growl or something.

I have no idea why, but a couple of minutes after I noticed the creature, it turned its whole body and faced somewhere off to its right. It was hard to tell whether something had caught its attention, or it was pretending like it was no longer interested in me. As soon as it turned like that, I immediately noticed it was slouching. It was difficult to ascertain if it had a hunchback or just terrible posture compared to the human standard. Call me crazy, but I wouldn't say I was frightened when seeing this thing for the first time. I was far more curious, and that feeling seemed mutual. I immediately knew that it was rare to see one; therefore, I wanted the moment to last. I didn't want it to run off before I could observe more of its features.

The visitor had left after one of the occasions where I lowered my gaze to screw pieces of wood together. It might've still been watching me from somewhere close by, but I could no longer see it. I kept wondering if it would reappear while I finished the birdhouse, but I eventually went inside for the night.

I called my wife and told her all about what had happened. Although she was intrigued, she seemed much more interested in the notion that I had found a new hobby of making birdhouses and loved the idea that I planned to gift them to the neighbors. She did suggest that I try to get a picture of the animal if it shows up again, but I got the sense that she thought my eyes had played tricks on me.

Curious to find out whether the animal might reappear, I went out to that same spot to work on the birdhouses a little after dawn the next day. I didn't see anything. But when I returned there later, around the same time I saw it the previous day, it was back, and it was in the same spot, staring at me from behind that same tree. It watched me for probably around ten minutes before it vanished. Later that night, I decided that I should attempt to feed it the next day. If this thing was going to come around regularly, I thought it'd be good to present myself as a friend. If I could get it to trust me, maybe I would be able to capture photos and even videos of it freely. Since I felt so lost in life at the time, it seemed like this whole thing could be part of a calling that would point me in the right direction. What if I could become known for introducing the world to the truth that these animals are out there with indisputable proof?

This occurred years before everyone had a cellphone equipped with a camera, so I had to make a trip to the store to get a disposable film camera. I went to a local grocery store and grabbed a couple of them, hoping that'd I'd eventually acquire the freedom to snap as many pictures as I pleased. I also grabbed a giant fruit platter since I didn't want to guess which ones the animal liked and end up getting it wrong.

I did the same routine as the past couple of days, going out to work on the birdhouses when the creature showed up. It didn't come around that day, and I had worried that it wouldn't come back. But it returned the following day.

Although I wasn't terrified of the animal, I wasn't yet willing to carry the fruit platter over to it. It didn't feel wise to walk toward it. It felt a little like I was degrading the creature, but I tossed some pieces of fruit toward the tree that it stood behind. At first, the animal didn't budge; it merely continued to stare at me. I don't even recall seeing it aim its

11

gaze at the ground to analyze the fruit, leading me to believe it was a failed attempt. But after I returned my focus to my crafts, the animal approached the fruit. It felt like I was seeing the thing for the first time. Until that point, I hadn't had an unobstructed view of it.

Its fur was all black. I didn't notice even an inch of any other color on it aside from the face, where the skin was a few shades lighter. I'd describe the skin as charcoal or dark grey. Although it was slouching, I estimated it was a few inches taller than me, and I was about 6'1" back then. Its eyes were black, giving them a hollow look. Something else that I thought was very strange was how I didn't notice its odor until it was within ten yards of me. It hit my nose out of nowhere, and it was pretty damn bad. It had a swampy scent— like the creature had spent hours rolling around in the mud on a hot and humid day.

I have no idea why, but its mouth appeared to dangle while it went from fruit to fruit. It almost looked like its jaw muscles were detached until each time that it started chewing, which wasn't long-lasting. Whatever was going on with its mouth looked extremely uncomfortable; however, it didn't seem to be experiencing any pain.

The fruit was scattered about the soil in various places, so I waited for the creature to get to one of the closer pieces so that I could get a better photo. You could say it was my instincts, but an internal voice warned me not to take the picture. I sat there with that thought for a few moments but ultimately decided to take the risk. I don't know if it was the flash or the camera's sound when I snapped the photo, but the creature went berserk. As it ran toward me, I thought it was about to rip me in half; instead, it threw one of the birdhouses, smashed the other, then flipped the workbench over, all while making some strange screeching noise that reminded me of a woman's scream. The soundwave was so dense that I'm convinced I could feel it. That alone was unlike anything I had ever experienced before; I didn't even know it was possible. I wanted to run out of there, but I was much more focused on protecting my eardrums.

Once I covered my ears, I slowly backed away as the creature continued its rampage. It ran around the area, constantly changing directions. That was when its movements reminded me of an upset monkey or chimpanzee, establishing my theory that these animals are within the primate family.

I remember sweating bullets as I slowly walked away from the angry animal. It felt as though every step could be my last. Even when I eventually made it to the house, I thought I was a dead man. I wanted to slap myself for not having had my car keys on me while outside. I should've had those in my pockets if things went south as they did. There were moments where I debated making a run for my car, but that would obviously involve going back outside, and the driveway wasn't right next to the house. To make things even more complicated, none of the windows in the place provided a view of the area where I had left the creature, but I could hear it was still flipping the hell out.

I carefully went from window to window and closed all the blinds. I thought that would be the smart thing to do if the animal came looking for me. I then sat at the kitchen table and tried to be as quiet as possible. My nerves felt like they would explode when it sounded like the screaming noise was getting closer. Once the crazed creature sounded like it was within maybe twenty yards of the house, I carefully stood up and walked over to the kitchen to grab the largest knife I could find. The idea of having to defend myself with that was beyond horrifying. Suddenly, everything I had been doing felt so crazy. What was I thinking trying to lure that large, unpredictable animal? It made me feel neglectful of my family. I had never felt so overheated in my life; the suspense of that moment was almost unbearable. I thought that freak would come barging inside, looking to kill me any second. Using that camera had really pissed it off, and it was out for vengeance.

But soon, the noise softened. It continued to dissipate while it ran off into the distance. That was a comforting feeling, but how could I be sure that it wouldn't come back? I must've waited for an hour or two before I finally built enough courage to go to my car. I desperately needed to get the hell out of there. Thankfully, I didn't travel there with an excess of belongings, so I quickly tossed all the necessities into my backpack and ran toward my vehicle.

Once I reached a fairly busy town, I stopped at a diner and called my wife to tell her what had happened. I still don't think she believed the extent of the whole thing, but she agreed to list the house for sale that same month. I felt obligated to tell the listing agent about the incident so that potential buyers would be aware that they were taking a risk, but I had trouble deciding how to word it. It seemed like anything I could say would make me sound insane. I explained how some large animal charged me from the woods in the evening, but it was too dark to tell what it was. I'm hoping that the listing agent relayed that information, but my instincts suggest she didn't since the house sold quickly. I suppose there's always the possibility that the buyer didn't care about the alleged danger.

After looking into it, I'm convinced that what I saw on our old property was the southeastern variation of the sasquatch typically referred to as *swamp apes* or *skunk apes*. Even though it was still a large beast, it appeared much thinner than what I read in eyewitness accounts about the western subspecies, which is reportedly barrel-chested much thicker overall. This creature was more chimpanzee-like with longer, toned but slender limbs.

I can't imagine why anyone would ever want to cross paths with one of these animals. There are just way too many opportunities for the interaction to go south.

-It Followed Our Horses-

Location: Suttons Bay, Michigan

Submitted by: Elise H.

When I was just a pre-teen, I experienced the scare of a lifetime. I grew up on a ranch, and there were many trails surrounding the property. We'd frequently ride our horses on those trails whenever there was nice weather to ensure they stayed fit.

21

Once June rolled around, my parents would offer weekend horseback riding tours, and they kept those going until it got too cold out—usually around late November.

This one evening, I was riding in front of my dad, and I vividly remember how I had asked him if I could have some money to get a Britney Spears concert ticket. He didn't respond. After asking him for the second or third time, I noticed he was also looking over his shoulder. His focus was on something big lurking about fifty feet behind us. Initially, I thought it was a bear because of the long snout and pointed ears. But shortly after I spotted it, it started to look more like a massive coyote. I wanted to ask Dad to clarify what the animal was, but I was too shocked to speak. Nothing made sense about what I was looking at.

Even though I felt mystified over what I saw, I wouldn't say that the animal appeared very aggressive. Yes, it was walking behind us, but there were several moments where I wondered whether it was genuinely interested in us. Sometimes it seemed like it was much more interested in sniffing the ground than keeping an eye on us. I thought it had veered away into the woods a few times but would then reappear a minute or two later. Once we made it back to the ranch, the long-snouted animal had seemingly stopped following us.

"Dad, what kind of animal was that?" I asked. "Was it a skinny bear?"

"You know, I'm not too sure," he replied. Something in his voice conveyed that he was a bit worried—like the sighting gave him a bad feeling. But when I asked him if he was scared, he insisted that there was no reason to worry.

The following morning, I woke up to my mom screaming to my dad about what she had just found. She was panicking. I tried to understand what she said, but her sobbing obstructed her annunciation. I began to panic, thinking that one of our dogs had died. One of our three dogs was very old at the time, and it wouldn't have been that surprising had he passed away in the middle of the night. My parents had even had a couple of discussions with me, doing what they could to prepare me for the inevitable. But after I got to the kitchen, I was relieved to see all three of our dogs moseying around.

Dad had made his way outside just moments before I got there, so I had to ask my still-crying mom about what had happened.

"What's wrong?" I asked, placing my hand on Mom's upper back. It was easy to tell she was debating how to word her response.

"Something attacked Indigo last night," she said. "I'm so sorry, sweety, but he's gone."

25

I didn't know what to say. Indigo was the horse my dad rode the previous day when we spotted the strange creature on the path. As far as I can remember, that was the first time I had ever experienced the overwhelming sensation of denial. All of our animals were so important to me, but it had always seemed that our horses were invulnerable. That must've had something to do with their size. And our horses were very young and healthy, so it hadn't been on my radar that anything awful might happen to them. I ran outside before Mom even had a chance to elaborate. I needed to see it for myself. I convinced myself that if I ran out to the stable, I'd find Indigo in his usual spot, as happy and healthy as ever.

Dad tried to stop me when he noticed me catching up to him, but I ran far enough around him to where he had no chance of intercepting me. Indigo wasn't inside the stable, but my eyes quickly landed on the wreckage. Either a horse had broken out of there in the middle of the night—or *something* had broken in. When Dad entered the stable behind me, I dashed toward the hole in the wall.

"Elise, stop!" he yelled, but I didn't listen. I needed to find Indigo.

I arrived at the edge of the fence, covered my nose, and dropped to my knees. Flies were already swarming the remains. Most of the fur had been stripped from the corpse, so I continued to deny it belonged to one of

27

our horses. Nearly the entirety of the ribcage lay exposed, and all organs were missing—the blood splatter surrounding the mess spread in all directions. There were what looked to be a few pieces of intestine or some other lengthy innards hanging upon a section of the fence, indicating that whatever had killed Indigo likely took some of the meat with it for a future meal.

Dad immediately turned me away from the scene when he arrived at my side. "Go back to your mother," he commanded. He was a burly ranchman, but he was holding back tears. Soon after I started walking back toward the house, Dad caught up to me. He didn't say why, but he probably decided it was too risky to allow me to walk back there alone. What if whatever had killed our horse was still lurking nearby? I did sort of feel like something was watching us, but that sensation easily could've come from the nonother than trauma from what I had just seen.

"I'm sorry, Sweety," Mom said multiple times after we made it back inside. I remember thinking it was strange how she kept apologizing to me. Her tone made me feel like she somehow thought the whole thing was her fault. I now realize she was merely expressing sympathy for not having prevented me from seeing the gruesome scene. Together, the three of us wept for a good half an hour. Dad kept getting up to pace in the kitchen while looking away from us. I think he felt it was his duty to hold it together, to be the one Mom and I could trust to stand up to danger, but there was no question that he missed his horse. We were always so passionate about our animals, constantly trying to ensure they were well-fed, fit, and received lots of love.

"It had to be that animal we saw on the trail," Dad said. "There are no other predators around here that would be capable of killing a horse like that."

Although I knew he had to be correct, it was still hard to imagine the long-snouted creature pulling something like that off. Don't get me wrong—it was big—but not the size of a grizzly bear or fully-grown tiger. Whatever had killed Indigo had to be absurdly strong to pull off that task. Based on our initial sighting, it was even hard to imagine that animal getting that aggressive. It was deranged and mysterious looking, but I didn't get the sense that it was overly aggressive or evil like you hear so many people say nowadays about dogmen. Still, I'm confident that that's what my father and I saw. Bear in mind that I didn't even learn about that term until years later, and I was shocked to learn that other people had seen similar creatures in Michigan and Canada.

Anyway, aside from the deep sadness my parents felt, they forced themselves to get it together so they could decide how they were going to make sure our other horses avoided a similar fate. My dad came up with this crazy idea that he would spend the night in the stable with his rifle ready for the creature to return, but both Mom and I refused to allow that. I don't know if my mom had accepted our story of what we had seen the previous day, but she wasn't willing to risk my father. I often think about how glad I am that she put her foot down. Otherwise, I might not have had a dad for much longer.

The only other thing they could think to do was call their friends, Jeff and Leslie, to look after our horses for a few days. It wasn't an immediate decision since the couple lived about thirty minutes away, and my parents didn't like to transport the horses via trailer unless it was absolutely necessary. Well, this turned out to be one of those situations. There were other ranchers closer by to us, but I think they charged a hefty amount to board our horses since we weren't close friends with them. My parents had a reciprocal agreement with Jeff and Leslie where they'd look after each other's horses when needed.

Luckily, we made it to Jeff and Leslie's property without any trouble. We even brought our dogs along for the quick road trip to ensure they were also safe. We didn't have any other animals to look after, so it helped our mental states to have all of them in one place. My dad told Jeff and Leslie about everything, including the weird animal we saw the previous day. We all hoped they'd have some insight into the phenomenon, but they were duped.

We made sure to return home before it got dark so that Dad could further examine the hole in the stable. Mom forced him to agree he would come inside for the night once the sun started to set. When he got back into the house, I was glad to hear that no predators had approached him. I kept worrying that Mom and I would suddenly hear him firing his rifle or yelling from getting attacked. I was so freaked out by Indigo's surprise death that I begged we keep most of the lights on throughout the night. Even though the idea of wasting electricity was one of my dad's biggest pet peeves, he agreed. He was probably more concerned about my mental state than the power bill—at least, for a few days.

I'll never forget the feeling of waking up to the sound of the phone ringing at around 4:45 AM. When I walked toward my parents' bedroom to listen to their conversation, I couldn't believe my ears. I thought I had to be in a nightmare, and I tried desperately to wake up from it. Leslie had called to inform us that one of our other horses, Dasher, had been attacked. Fortunately, Jeff used his shotgun to scare the "dog-like" animal away before it could finish the killing, but Dasher was severely injured. Leslie suggested we head over there to say our goodbyes because she thought there was a good chance that they wouldn't be able to stop the bleeding in time.

Even though we were one of the very few people on the road at that time, the drive there felt like it lasted years. Both Mom and I were still in our pajamas because we just couldn't bring ourselves to care enough about our outfits at that moment to change them. Once we arrived at Jeff and Leslie's, we quickly learned of the most dreaded outcome—Dasher was no longer with us.

"Dasher and Indigo got their wings," Mom said, holding me close. "They got their wings."

How was it possible that this animal tracked down our other horse? Not only did it have to have possessed the world record for the best sense of smell, but also determination. Why was it so hellbent on killing our horses? That aspect makes me wonder if these creatures are indeed demonic or satanic. As nutty as that must sound to some, it's so hard to make sense of them otherwise. That thing had followed us for all that distance— all while appearing uncaring of us— suddenly made everything about it so much creepier. It decided its targets and then went after both of them within the following 48 hours—even though one of the horses was a thirty-minute drive away. It's difficult to imagine anything more bloodthirsty than that. I have to confess that there's no way we can know 100% whether it was the same creature that we saw on the trail, but Jeff's description matched it entirely.

Understandably, it was easy to tell that Jeff and Leslie were in disbelief about everything that had just happened. Just as our family did, they tried to develop a more logical explanation. Jeff said the creature ran on two legs but had the head of a husky. He thought it looked just like a werewolf. When Dad and I saw the beast, it must've only been moving on all fours to sniff the ground more easily. What was it doing? Is it possible that it was smelling the soil where the horses had just stepped, determining whether it wanted to pursue them as food? Everything about what had happened made me yearn for the strange animal to go away. I never wanted to see it again or hear about it attacking anyone else's beloved pets. I wished so badly that it would die. It's the only time I can ever think of when I wanted to kill. I wanted revenge for the overwhelming sadness I felt.

Jeff and Leslie were kind enough to provide their guestroom for my parents and me to get some more rest. Although it was still dark outside, I don't think any of us were able to fall back asleep; we were much too disturbed by the recent events.

It wasn't long after the sun came up that I heard my dad do his best to sneak out of the room. He and Jeff chatted somewhere down the hall, and then I heard them head outside. I remember thinking it was amazing how either one of them felt okay being out there knowing that a werewolf-like beast was roaming the vicinity. A part of me hoped that my dad and Jeff encountered the creature so that one of them could shoot it. It seemed safer to try to kill it while they were together instead of alone. But a lack of audible gunshots indicated that the mysterious animal wasn't around. Jeff and Leslie's property was wide-open, so I felt comfortable knowing that nothing would have the luxury of being able to sneak up on anyone before getting blasted.

Our families worked together to find a place hours away to board our horses until we felt safe again. Jeff and my dad spoke over the phone often for the next few weeks, hoping to receive updates from one another. Strangely enough, none of us came across any further clues that the werewolf-like beast was still around. I thought we might hear some strange sounds in the middle of the night, but there was nothing out of the ordinary.

My mom did file a police report, and I'm pretty sure Jeff or Leslie did in their county, but neither of our families received any updates as far as I know. I don't think any of us ever met anyone else who claimed to have seen the creepy creature.

If you live in the Midwest and wander outside often, be sure to keep an eye out. Thanks for providing me with a decent outlet to share my account. I sincerely hope we can one day find out exactly what these animals are and where they came from.

-The Creepy Facility-

Location: Idyllwild, California

Submitted by: Gary B.

Although it's not the longest story, I sure do have a strange one. My wife and I lived in Idyllwild for the first eighteen years of our marriage, and it was close to the end of that period that we were out walking on one of our usual trails and saw something so freaky that I sometimes still have trouble accepting that it happened.

It was one of the muddier spring days we had seen. I remember how we almost backed out of going for our daily walk, but we had recently started an intense weight loss regimen and didn't want to cheat ourselves out of progress. The trailhead was about a five-minute drive from where we lived. Even though we walked on this trail often, we usually turned around when we arrived at a sharp incline that you could use to get to the top of a mountain. My wife, Connie, had a bit of a hip problem back then, and it would ache if she did anything too strenuous. But she said she was feeling ambitious that day and wanted to keep going.

Eventually, you would get to a point on the trail where you could see a large grey facility that didn't have any windows and was surrounded by a tall barbed-wire fence. Neither of us thought much of it, assuming it was just some boring electrical building. The facility had to have been a solid 100 yards from the fence. There were plenty of trees in the middle, making the building difficult to see once everything had bloomed for summer.

It was the first hike where the facility caught my lasting attention. There was a gigantic rip in a section of the fence close to the trail. I kid you not when I say it looked like a giant had peeled it apart with its massive hands. Something about the scene felt very off—like something remarkably unusual had occurred. There was also an odd smell in the air, but it wasn't uncommon to come across the scent of a decaying animal in those parts. Wildlife was everywhere. I wasn't sure if we should keep walking, but Connie felt so enthusiastic that day that she was determined to keep going. Initially, she didn't seem too concerned about the break in the fence. She merely assumed some large buck had gotten its antlers caught in it and eventually managed to pull the thing apart to free itself.

We didn't stick around long, but we ran into a brigade of armed men after we continued up the path. They were dressed in camouflage and were carrying high-caliber automatic weapons. Since I had never seen anything like that around there, I asked the men what was happening.

"Move along," one of them replied.

I explained that I just wanted a simple explanation for whether there was potential danger in the area where we reside. Still, the same gentleman disregarded my question and suggested we head back toward our car. Since the group looked serious, my wife and I agreed it was best to return home.

"What in tarnation do you think that was all about?" my wife asked me once we were far enough away from the crew of soldiers.

"Who can say?" I said. But I wouldn't be surprised if it had to do with that busted fence."

We heard footsteps behind us when we were about halfway back to the car. My wife and I turned around simultaneously, expecting to see a fellow hiker who had caught up to us, but it was something else entirely.

My wife shrieked when we locked eyes with the being that had to have been at least eight feet tall. It had all black hair with olive-colored skin visible on its face, hands, and feet. We couldn't believe our eyes.

Although we spotted it, the tall figure maintained the same pace as it walked toward us. The only time it broke eye contact was once when it checked to see if anyone or anything was following it, and that was when I noticed it had to turn its entire torso. The neck on this thing was close to nonexistent. In all my life, I've never seen something so muscular. I can't even begin to imagine the strength that it must've possessed. That aspect alone was one of the most disturbing things I've ever encountered. We were walking down a ridge when we spotted the massive creature, and all we could really do was step to the side and get out of the way, hoping it would leave us alone.

After we stepped out of the way, it got down on all fours and ran like a large cat. It was that light on its feet. Before we knew it, it was out of sight. Its speed was incomprehensible. I don't understand how anything can run that fast, especially something that appeared to have human DNA.

Due to that encounter and the broken fence, my wife and I believe that that building was some sort of secret government building—perhaps one where they conduct experiments on things most of us don't know exist.

I've read about so many different types of bigfeet in countless encounter reports; therefore, I can't be 100% sure that what ran by us was a sasquatch in the traditional sense. For all we know, this thing was some twisted experiment gone wrong, and the subject broke out of the facility. That's my theory. But who's to say that the laboratory wasn't cloning bigfeet or something of the sort? The more I think about it, the more bizarre possibilities I come up with.

In any case, my wife and I are so grateful that the creature didn't attack us. There would've been absolutely nothing we could do to prevent an animal like that from taking our lives. One swipe from something that size would be enough to knock a man's head clean off his shoulders. No wonder there was a whole brigade of armed soldiers searching for the thing. I'm sure that even they would find it challenging to take one of the creatures out.

It sure is a strange world that we live in. I feel great sympathy for all the folks who have encountered these things but didn't live to talk about them. There needs to be more transparency around this subject.

-Fly Fishing Fury-

Location: Idaho

Submitted by: Brandon T.

When I was in grade school, my mom's ex-boyfriend took me on a fly-fishing trip up in Idaho. His name was Dan, and he was very passionate about fishing. He also saw it as a way for us to grow closer. He was a pretty nice guy, but I think his primary intention was for my mom to invest in him more than she already had. I believe that he could tell she was sort of on the rocks about staying with him, so he looked at me like I was a direct link to her heart. Perhaps if I had many good things to say about him, I would relay them to my mom, and she would decide that he was worth staying with after all. I doubt most mothers would appreciate their significant other running off and leaving their child to deal with a monster.

Seeing as how I was only eleven years old, it was the earliest I had ever woken up when Dan tapped me on the shoulder while it was still dark outside. I so badly wanted to keep sleeping, but I've always been one of those agreeable types, so I did as he requested. The guy was such an avid fisherman that he whispered when talking to me, even though we were at least 200 yards from the river. It was like he was convinced that the fish would be able to hear us from that far away and might swim off. When I think back on it, I think the guy was a little kooky. Yeah, there's no question about that. I can't believe I'm only just realizing that now.

It was drizzling when we arrived at the river, so I think that's part of why we were the only ones there. All that did was make Dan even happier to be out there. As you might've guessed, we weren't allowed to talk while casting. I think he believed we would bond just by standing there next to one another in silence. One of the only times that he spoke to me while we were at the river was when he explained that I wouldn't catch anything by sitting on a boulder. He said that posture was everything, and I needed to stand to get a nice fluid motion going while casting my line.

It wasn't long after he corrected me that the mysterious figure appeared. It was hunched over and standing on a ridge overlooking the river from the opposite side. Therefore, I would estimate it was maybe forty to fifty yards away from us. The sunlight was still dim by that point, making it tricky to discern its features in detail. But I will say that there were moments when it looked more apelike and other times when it appeared more man-like. Whatever it was, it looked elderly. There were many patches of grey and white hair all over it. I had heard of Bigfoot by that point, but this thing looked different than how I had ever imagined the supposed creature of legend to look. Even though the siding was downright shocking, I wasn't as scared as I should've been. The water was moving pretty fast, and the cliff where the creature stood had to be at least 25 feet above. I didn't expect it to feel inclined to dive in, so I assumed we were safe. That doesn't imply that I didn't want to move away from the area as soon as possible. It's just that I didn't feel we were in any immediate danger.

I felt tempted to ask Dan what was staring at us from the cliff, but I had already been warned not to talk, so I did as I was told. He was standing a good 50 feet to my right, so I would've had to shower in his direction anyway. I kept expecting him to walk over and see me, but it was like the creature hypnotized him. I don't think he knew what to do.

The mysterious figure suddenly went from seeming relaxed and curious to startled and aggressive. It held its long arms above its head, hooting and hollering like a total lunatic. Things only got weirder when it started urinating off the cliff before us. It must've been a territorial act, but it happened before I understood any of that.

Soon after the creature started flipping out, I smelled the most disgusting odor ever to touch my nose. I don't think it was the scent of the urine, though; it smelled more like a dead skunk that had been baking atop pavement on a hot summer day. It was the most atrocious thing I've ever experienced to this day. Mere words don't have any chance of doing it justice.

Right after the figure finished urinating everywhere, it leaped into the water. The creature went from seeming a bit bulky and clumsy to lean and limber within an instant. It got so much hangtime in the air and looked so graceful. I feel like I'm making it sound like I was watching the creature for an extensive period. That's not at all the case. Everything that I just explained happened within maybe 45 seconds of it appearing.

Believe it or not, Dan had already started running away before he even yelled at me to get out of there. If you're an adult and looking after a child, that's pretty embarrassing behavior. After the creature dove into the water, it stayed underneath the surface until I fled from the area. Therefore, I had no idea whether it was swimming toward my position or where Dan had been standing. I know that it didn't drown because I heard it screaming when I was on my way back to camp. Can you even begin to imagine being a child and hearing that man-like animal's creepy noises echoing from nearby?

Do you want to know what's even more pathetic about Dan? He was waiting inside his vehicle with the doors locked when I arrived at our camp. The engine was on, leaving me to wonder if he had decided that I was dead meat, and there was no point in waiting around to see if I would return. I want to clarify that I don't think he was an evil man with ill intentions, but I believe he was the biggest wimp around. It's more than understandable to be afraid of these mysterious creatures; it's another thing to leave a child to fend for themselves. We ended up leaving all of his camping and fishing gear behind.

I wonder what he would've told my mom had I not made it back to the car. Can you even begin to imagine that situation? I kind of felt bad when I told her all about what happened, and she assumed it was a bear or some typical predator and not a sasquatch, but Dan and I will always know the truth. That's, at least, one thing we had in common. I wish I still had his contact information so that I could talk to him about it now in my adult years.

It would be fascinating to hear his take on the whole thing. I wonder if he might pretend to have forgotten about it due to the embarrassment of having left his girlfriend's kid behind. Anyway, that's the gist of my story. I genuinely wish there was a way to inform the world that this species is among us. I think every person on the planet has the right to know. If only there were a way to make it indisputable.

-Down the Well-

Location: Pacific Northwest

Submitted by: Richard Hunt (Author)

L ess than two years ago, the station dispatched me to someone's ranch house in the middle of the afternoon. It was an extraordinary circumstance. A housekeeper had called the police, claiming to have witnessed a muscular old man of around eight feet tall intruding on the property and throwing the owner down his well. She said the homeowner was still down there and not responding to the maid's calls. Given the variety of strange things I had seen up to that point, I had suspicions about what we were dealing with.

Nobody was in sight when I pulled up to the house, and I was surprised to find that it took the housekeeper a long time to make her way down the steps. I was about to kick the door in when it finally opened, revealing a terrified woman in her thirties. I quickly learned that English was not her first language, making our communication shaky. You would think that anyone in a panicked situation would race down to the door to meet the police after they call for them. But it quickly became apparent that she was worried about who or *what* might be on the other side of the door.

She told me she could barely hear the doorbell from inside the walk-in closet where she hid. And there was no window on that side of the house to view my parked squad car. Whatever this woman had seen, she seemed to assume the aggressor would be capable of understanding how doorbells function. Therefore, it couldn't just be any typical predator. But how often do we come across people near eight feet tall—especially when talking about elderly folks? Sure, the witness couldn't describe the culprit as accurately as she wanted, but there was that unmistakable look of trauma all over her face. I could tell she had seen something from another world.

Eventually, I got her to point in the direction of the well. I got the impression that she was confused about why even a police officer would want to head over there to check things out. When I think back on the situation, she might've been confused about why the department would only send one police officer over. Not all operators know the reality behind these sasquatch encounters, so there's a good chance that whatever she had said over the phone wasn't taken seriously by the individual in charge of dispatching officers. The story probably sounded a little too exaggerated to them—like maybe the caller suffered from delusions; therefore, they didn't want to waste many resources. Basically, there's a good chance I was summoned to verify that the absurd claim didn't hold any truth.

The well was located behind the house, maybe a hundred yards away, and close to the dense forest edge. Since it was a scorching summer day, I figured a sasquatch might've been searching for water. It had probably come across this well or others in the past and learned that they often contain water. The property had many acres, so that would've been understandable had a stealth creature wandered about the area undetected before that point.

As I arrived at the well, I could immediately tell that the thing was ancient, undoubtedly having seen several generations of residents.

"Hello? Is anyone down there? Can you hear me?" I yelled as I arrived at the edge of the well. The sun was so bright that day, rendering it impossible to see anything at the bottom. Even my flashlight didn't provide any assistance in reducing the glare. I believe it was cicadas that were as noisy as ever that day, making it difficult to hear anything that might've been occurring at the bottom of the well. I began to imagine a scenario where a man was truly down there alive, yet too weak from injury to shout for help.

I circled the edge of the well a few times, shining my flashlight at various angles, hoping to get any visual that would prompt me to summon the paramedics, but no luck. Suddenly, I heard a scuffling coming from down the well. Hoping that it might be the homeowner regaining consciousness, I called out his name once more. Nothing could've prepared me for what happened next. The hairy brute missed me by inches, flying right past my face as it leaped out of the well. I never got an exact explanation for how deep that well went, but judging by how I couldn't see anything by merely looking down into it, I estimate it to have been over 80 feet.

The creature that hopped out was so large that I don't understand how it could fit down there. The circumference must have been just beyond the width of its shoulders. Within seconds, I could immediately tell why the housekeeper perceived it to be an older man. There were gray streaks everywhere throughout its fur, and its Caucasian color face was wrinkly and worn. The beast landed on the other side of the well but turned and snarled at me. That was when I saw the markings of fresh blood on its teeth and around its lips. I didn't get a direct look at its hands due to being distracted by the danger, but I'm sure they were also soaked in blood. It couldn't have been more apparent that this animal had jumped down into the well after tossing the man in it. I suppose it decided that it couldn't waste an easy meal of fresh meat.

Although the creature was massive, as always, I could tell that it was malnourished. It appeared to be in a state where it was tempted to take any available option to give it energy. But even though it was likely much weaker than usual, there's no question that it could've ripped me to pieces in mere seconds. There are just no two ways about it. Luckily, the creature began running away before I could draw my gun. I still don't think my bullets would've been enough to take the beast down if it got aggressive with me. I would've been a goner.

Although the beast had fled, it was my duty to call the station and inform one of my supervisors what had happened. Within less than ten minutes, backup had arrived. I watched as the fire department used some special tool to lift the remains of the homeowner out of the well. Even though the man was missing a lot of his flesh, I could still see that he was older than I had imagined. I wouldn't be surprised if the creature decided that this guy was on the brink of death anyway, so why not consume his remaining nutrients?

The housekeeper was so traumatized that she refused to step out of the house unless officers surrounded her. I didn't have a whole lot more to do with that case. After returning to the station and filling out the case file on my computer, other "more qualified" personnel took things from there. I don't doubt that professionals were assigned to hunt down the malnourished creature and terminate it. The real question is, were there any human casualties along the way? That's something that the department would never disclose to anyone who isn't actively involved in the case.

-Real Wolfmen-

Location: Addison, Michigan

Submitted by: Sarah M.

Hi, I'm Sarah. I grew up in a very small Michigan town known as Addison. For most of my teenage years, I was the prime babysitter in the area. Every parent with small children would call me to come over to look after their little ones. Because of that, I was, hands-down, the richest teenager around. I remember how other kids my age tried to do the same thing, but they could never build the same reputation. It was great, but don't get me wrong; even the most pleasant jobs can almost get you killed.

One of my most frequent clients was a little boy named Eric. His mother was a widow who had recently started dating after nearly three years of trying to get over her husband's death. She was in her late 20s and extremely beautiful, so every bachelor within the vicinity asked her out. On top of the frequent money, Eric was one of the easier-going kids I looked after. It was always a breeze. He never screamed or complained when I asked him to finish his vegetables, brush his teeth, get to bed, etc. He was delightful.

But one night, his mother explained to me that he had been a little freaked out the past few days. Eric claimed he had seen a werewolf looking at him through his window in the middle of the night, two nights in a row. Eric's mother assumed he must have recently seen a werewolf while watching TV, which scared him out of his wits. When I asked him about it, he told me that he did not see any werewolves on television. Nothing strange came about on that particular night, but I believe it was only a couple of weeks later that Eric and I were reading a book in his backyard gazebo when it appeared. It seemingly came out of nowhere, and something about the deranged look of this thing made me feel as though my soul had briefly left my body. It was so strange to look at—like something straight out of the creepiest of nightmares. The tall ears and long snout combined with human-like eyes were enough to give many people a heart attack.

What's interesting is how Eric's reaction to the encounter was delayed. He seemed too terrified to scream after finding out that the creature was near. But it was as soon as the beast took one more step toward us that the little boy screamed louder than I've ever heard anyone else. It felt like we were in one of the worst possible places to be during an encounter with a large Apex predator. There was nothing to separate us from the sharp claws and teeth other than a combination of thin wood and wired screening. I thought it was for sure getting ready to come after us—like it was thinking it had finally gotten Eric into a position where he wouldn't be able to get away. Unknowing what else to do, I picked the little boy up to try to comfort him.

While he wept on my shoulder, I scanned our surroundings for anything that could be used as a weapon. The only object within reaching distance was the rock they used to hold the flimsy gazebo doors shut amid windy days. But even if I were given adequate time to step outside to fetch it, it would probably be too heavy for me to do anything with it.

All I could think to do at the moment was calm Eric, hoping that that might calm the situation—and maybe the creepy animal would eventually lose interest. I didn't want to shout and try to intimidate the animal, for I was worried that might make it hostile.

"It's okay," I whispered to the little boy, trying to convince myself just as much as him. "It's okay. There's nothing to worry about."

I tried to avoid eye contact with the creature, but my peripheral vision indicated it was sniffing the air. I started to wonder why it hadn't yet attacked. Did it not know that it was more than capable of breaking into the gazebo and snatching both of us simultaneously? Doing so would be effortless for something of that size.

The wolflike creature took another half step toward the gazebo before commotion in the surrounding woods caught its attention. It turned around and saw a couple of deer just before I did. I watched as its ears perked up, much like what you see when something excites a domesticated dog. The animal was upon the doe within an instant, its teeth penetrating the throat.

Since the gazebo didn't provide much protection, I dashed out of there with Eric still in my arms. There was a moment while I was sprinting when I heard a hair-raising roar that made it sound like the creature was approaching us, but when I turned around, I could see that it was still feasting in the woods. When we made it into the house, I made sure all the doors were locked. I then called the police and informed them that there was a highly dangerous beast in the backyard—one that I couldn't identify.

A couple of policemen arrived between five and ten minutes later and proceeded toward the backyard to check things out. I anxiously waited with Eric in the den, expecting to hear a gunshot or two, but there was nothing. I felt tempted to sneak over to one of the windows so that I could glimpse whatever was happening, but I didn't want to leave the troubled little boy's sight, and I didn't want to bring him near any of the windows because it was clear that he had seen enough of the monster.

Eventually, the police informed me that they found the deer carcass, but the killer was nowhere to be found. Both men seemed to be shaken by whatever they saw out there. I don't think either of them knew of any predator capable of stripping nearly all the flesh from an adult deer within that brief period. After all, Michigan isn't exactly known for large and ferocious carnivores. They were so perplexed by the doe's remains that they had the animal control department come pick everything up.

I assumed they took the leftover meat to some laboratory to run some tests and that Eric's mother would receive a phone call with some updates. I stopped coming around their house due to overwhelming fear, and I never heard any updates as to whether the police or anyone had called back. I did, however, get the impression that Eric's mom was a bit irritated by my unwillingness to continue working for her, so she probably wouldn't have let me in on any updates even if they had provided her with extensive information.

I'm convinced that Eric and I encountered a dogman. What dogmen are, I have no clue. It looked like a wolfman, and it would have no trouble taking the life of an unarmed person wandering in the woods. For about a year after that, I tried to avoid going outside with any of the kids I babysat. It's strange how I never met anyone else who claimed to have seen anything like it. That makes me think these are some of the rarest, most secretive animals on this planet.

-The Hairy Bullies-

Location: Douglass Falls Grange Park, Washington

Submitted by: Anonymous

Hello, I'm from a small town in Washington called Kettle Falls, and that's where I experienced one of the biggest regrets of my life. I was by myself during the incident, so I didn't know what else to do other than run. I was only 17 years old, but I wonder if I could've done something to help prevent the fatality. It happened over sixteen years ago, and I've told very few people about it due to embarrassment for not having been braver.

It was a weekend in spring, and I had a nasty fight with my high school sweetheart the previous night. Her name was Cassie, and I was livid after seeing her flirt with another guy while at a friend's party. I wasn't quite sure how to go about it, so I decided to go for a hike, hoping to clear my head. It's a beautiful place that I had visited with my parents ever since I was a child, and being there had always had a way of soothing my thoughts.

I had just made it to the edge of a clearing when I began to hear the cries for help. I remember I paused my stride because I was having trouble detecting where the noise was coming from, but it wasn't long before I saw an individual in a bright orange raincoat emerge from the woods. There was a dense meadow between us, but I could see her holding onto her hood, trying to shield her head. I then watched as the woman grabbed her back, wincing in pain. She was still too far away, but I could tell some projectile hit her torso. Whatever nailed her slowed her down momentarily, but she soon returned to full speed.

It wasn't long before I noticed the woman was holding a camera in one hand, and then I saw what was chasing her. Out of the woods came not one but two hairy beings. One was moving on two legs, the other on four. Initially, I thought the duo was a man and his off-leash dog, but that perception went right out the window when I watched the four-legged creature rise to two feet.

When the fleeing woman turned her head and saw that the duo had come out of the woods and was moving in her direction, she began screaming louder than ever. She had gone hysterical. Beyond puzzled, I watched one of the creatures pick up what had to be stone and hurl it at the terrified woman. The throwing motion of the animal was so bizarre, leading me to think that the joint and muscle placement is different from ours. They started throwing small stones, but eventually, one of the creatures picked up a much larger rock and threw it with impressive velocity. It appeared to land somewhere on the back of the woman's leg, and she instantly collapsed, screaming the loudest yet. She tried to stand up but quickly fell over, indicating that at least one of her bones was broken.

Her falling over seemed to excite the creatures, and they quickly hopped toward her, hollering like a couple of savage lunatics. They took turns slamming their giant fists onto the woman's torso, and it wasn't long before she fell silent. They continued to beat her limp body, and I finally realized that I should get out of there as quickly as possible.

After I had begun walking along the path back toward the car, the strange hollering stopped, making me extremely nervous. I could no longer keep track of their whereabouts. How was I supposed to know if they might've sniffed me out and had already initiated the hunt? Any moment, I might feel the sensation of a stone piercing my skin.

After arriving at the parking lot, I had never felt so grateful to enter my vehicle. I told my family what had happened as soon as I got home. My parents weren't sure what to make of it, but they had me call the police. All I could tell the authorities was that a woman was battered by a couple of strange individuals while in the woods. I tried to inform them of where I witnessed it, and they said they'd send people to check things out. We never heard anything back. I've always wondered if those hairy bullies cleaned up any trace of the murder or if the police purposefully avoided telling us about their findings.

I'll always regret that I couldn't help save that woman's life. It took me so long to get used to the fact that I had watched a murder happen and didn't do a thing to intervene. There are many courageous people out there who would've put their lives on the line. I was just too young, too afraid, and too unfamiliar with what I was looking at. Everything about the situation made me freeze up.

I believe the sasquatches went after her because they interpreted the camera as a weapon, but who knows? Thank you for taking an interest in my story. People need to take these creatures more seriously.

-THE FORBIDDEN REPORT-

Location: Munising, Michigan

Submitted by: Kathy B.

WARNING: Due to the gruesome nature of this report, it didn't feel right to include it in this book. It is terribly disturbing. If you'd still like your FREE copy, please visit this link:

http://eepurl.com/hQ6Y1f

More Sightings

If you're looking for more **Bigfoot-related content,** don't hesitate to check out books by Tom Lyons. He was a big help with showing me how to publish my stories!

Author's Request

I can't tell you how much I appreciate you taking the time to read my book. If you enjoyed it, I would be very grateful if you could leave a short and sweet review on Amazon.

Social Media

If you'd like to interact with me via social media, please follow my Instagram account:

 @BigfootAndDogman

Author Bio

Richard Hunt lives an unusual life. He currently works as a police officer in the Pacific Northwest and had his first bigfoot sighting while on the job. The experience disturbed him unlike anything else he had ever experienced, birthing his newfound belief that the world needs to know these creatures exist.

But there lies a challenge with this agenda: many of the good people who have worked in law enforcement in bigfoot-populated areas are aware of the coverup and the consequences that can come with trying to expose it. For that reason, "Richard Hunt" is not the author's real name but rather an alias to help protect his career.

Richard believes there's an advantage to his new hobby of writing: it'll enable him to inform readers of the most remarkable sasquatch-related incidents—all of which government does not want you to know.

Printed in Great Britain
by Amazon